Printed in the United States of America


First Printing, 2018

Blaze Publishing

1000 Newstead Avenue St. Louis, Mo.

63110

*For Him and Blaze*

*And the nameless 60 million-plus since Roe vs. Wade*

My undying thanks to:

Fred, my amazing husband

who made writing a book possible.

Garen, my wonderful son who mandated the outline

that

revealed the purpose— you made publishing a reality.

Jesse, my precious daughter who insisted I could do

better and passionately reveled in words with me.

Pat, who always encouraged and pushed those hard

re-writes.

Inez, who gave me the title.

*HALLELUJAH*

*ANYWAY*

*Jeanne Lafser*

Chapter 1

**Sam Gafner was Greek-god handsome**, a

self-proclaimed bohemian, and a big shot. He brought

buffalo back to Missouri, a riverboat to town, and dined

with President Jimmy Carter at the White House. He

lived alone in a loft above the florist shop he'd

purchased for his wife who abandoned the gift soon

after opening day, along with their marriage of four

years. But Sam kept the shop anyway.

These things—and *everything* about Sam Gafner

caused people to speculate and women to flock.

Instinctively, I disliked this obnoxiously overt man and

was grateful I would never encounter him, because

even though Jefferson City, Missouri was a small town,

Sam Gafner and I lived in very separate worlds. He was a cocky outsider running with the trendy young governor's staff, who, by their own assessment, were born to maintain planetary orbits and keep the unwashed masses in line as well. To me, they were power-crazy glad-handers and I hoped never to be one.

However, the need for income trumped my nasty little attitude and I found myself getting just what I deserved—a job selling ads at a weekly tabloid which covered Missouri politics of all things. With my fur rubbed the wrong way, so to speak, I was further humiliated because I was an utter failure at sales. In three months I'd only sold one tiny ad—to my brother who felt sorry for me. Fortunately, however, I had made it known that my true desire was to write and so

I was increasingly offered assignments. My great hope was for a byline, even though writing about politics repulsed me. So, it was a humorous little irony when this soul-wrenching job intersected my life with the annoying Sam Gafner.

It happened that my first big story was scheduled to be the feature article one particular week. On the morning of the edition's release, I raced to work early to see the issue and my byline. As I grabbed a folded paper from the drop bin and flipped it to full spread, my heart pounded hard against my chest with excitement. But then it stopped. There, staring at me from a black and white photograph, under a big, fat headline that was supposed to be mine, was Sam Gafner! My mind was a frenzy of questions:

how had this happened? Where was my article? I

quickly flipped through all the pages. Nothing. I

immediately went to ask my editor what happened.

"I'm so sorry, Effie!" Marta apologized. "Late last

night, we got wind of more activity on the dioxin issue.

It trumps everything. I promise your article will run

next week."

One had to trust Marta's judgment and sincerity. I

thanked her and slunk down the empty halls to the

break room. It was still so early, no one was there. I

dropped in a chair, compelled to read the article

despite my disappointment. Instead, I found myself

staring at Sam's photograph. He certainly was

handsome. Movie-star handsome. I'd never seen him

before and found myself just sitting and admiring his

face.  Shocked at myself, I finally covered the photo with my hand and focused on the article.

Marta had written it and done a great job describing the issues surrounding this volatile political controversy: the removal and disposal of highly toxic soil from a tiny town in Missouri.  The unnerving discovery of deadly toxins had recently attracted nationwide attention, including feature stories in *TIME Magazine* and *USA TODAY*.  Sam was quoted throughout the piece, as the director of the state agency overseeing the whole mess in conjunction with the Environmental Protection Agency at the federal level.

To my utter surprise, Sam's insights into the complexities and sensitivities of this political hotbed were profound and incisive.  His comments revealed an extensive knowledge of the issues at hand.

Furthermore, he masterfully addressed all the opposing

concerns with one viable solution.  His was the voice of

reason above the fray.  *Who would have thought the*

*gadfly had a brain?*  I had to admit I was intrigued and a

bit humbled by this new data. Nevertheless, I persisted

in disliking Sam Gafner.  There were already many

negative neural pathways regarding him.  One news

article couldn't change that.  Brilliant or not, I still

wanted nothing to do with this upstager who,

unbeknownst to me, was a meteorite about to crash

into my world again—but this time, in person.

Chapter 2


**Unbelievably, the very next day,** my ad manager asked

me to cold-call Sam's florist shop.  No one had been

able to secure an account with him, so it was my turn

fail—I mean try.  I was instantly horrified and angry.  I

didn't voice my thoughts, but Joe Ryan, my larger-than-

life Irish boss, could tell I was upset.  He yanked his

reading glasses off his face and stared bug-eyed at me

from across his desk.

"Why Effie, you look like a bristled hyena!  Wipe that

scowl off your face and go sell your second ad for

crying out loud!"

"Yes Sir." I replied respectfully, but all I could think

about was how Big Shot Sam Gafner had just stolen my

moment of glory, and now I must go grovel before him!

Trying to calm myself, I surmised that surely I would

meet with one of Sam's employees instead of him and

this greatly consoled me.

Yet, for two days I deferred making contact with

anyone at the flower shop. I did this with all my sales

calls—wrestling hard with ferocious procrastination.

But the day always came when it was time to call or be

fired—and so it was with Sam Gafner's flower shop.

It was a beautiful spring morning when I finally

mustered the courage to make the dreaded visit. To

my utter surprise, I put on mascara and fussed over

which skirt was more flattering. Clearly, the possibility

of running into Sam was on my mind.

As I walked from the newspaper office, only two blocks away, I happened to catch my reflection in a storefront window. Such surprise viewings always made me self-conscious in those days. It was because I didn't resemble the bulk of the local female population who were predominately of German (Arian) ancestry. I was not petite and loaded with blonde hair. Nor was I tan with white, piano-key teeth, sky-blue eyes, and well-developed calf muscles. On the contrary, I was tall, slender, dark-haired with grey-blue eyes and marginally white teeth. My skin was fair and prone to sunburn and freckles. I had long body parts: a long neck, long legs, long arms, long fingers, and a long waist. I was a quirky blend of Irish, English, Cherokee Indian, and African American (by rumor or reality, no one was sure). I always wished my feet were smaller like those of the truly German girls, and for years I bought shoes one size too small, certain that by force my feet would shrink. Instead they ached, and ultimately I succumbed to size nine (and-a-half).

Despite all this inconsistency with the prevailing phenotype, I accepted my body. Relocating, after all, was not an option. Besides, it had housed me all these years and so I felt an affectionate kinship with it. What Sam Gafner would think, however, I could not imagine.

As it happened, I walked into the flower shop, introduced myself to the clerk at the counter, explained I was from *The Review*, and asked to see Mr. Gafner.

"Let me buzz him and see if he has a minute," she said.

There was a quick exchange and then she turned to me. "He wants you to go on up. And by the way, no one calls him Mr. Gafner. Just call him Sam."

"Up?!" I blurted out in utter horror. "To his loft? I'm meeting HIM!?!" The clerk looked surprised and slightly irritated. "You did ask to speak with him. He's only got a few minutes—so if you've changed your mind..."

"Oh! No—no, I need to see him. Thank you." She pointed toward the stairs, and I began the climb to meet the man I had hoped to avoid. At the top of the steps, I stopped. The large loft-like room was dimly lit by a long row of dirty windows framed in rusted metal. I squinted in the smeary light but saw no one.

"Sam?"

No response.

"Mr. Gafner?"

"Yes. I'm over here. Please have a seat," a pleasant voice instructed.

I looked around the cluttered room. There in a corner, seated at a huge antique roll-top desk was the dark-haired, strikingly handsome, Sam Gafner. He wore blue jeans and a soft-looking, faded, denim shirt which contradicted his intense, serious presence. He was so deeply absorbed in whatever was on the desk that he didn't look up. As I walked closer, Sam still stared at his papers, and said again, "Have a seat."

I looked around. There was not a chair in sight. Just boxes.

"Please, make yourself comfortable." he persisted, still engrossed in his work.

"I'll just—I'll stand if you don't mind." I offered, not wanting to embarrass him with the telling fact that *there was no chair*. Still, no eye contact.

Then Sam started scribbling with great intensity, as though amending the Constitution. Suddenly he stopped and looked just past me.

"Would you be interested in buying this desk and chair?" he asked. "They go together, and I believe they're each over 100 years old. The top still works perfectly."

Sam stood up and tugged at the edge of the top section, hidden inside the beautiful walnut casing. He tugged again and again.

"I think it's stuck," he commented as he grappled to unleash the roll top. Then, it suddenly sprung loose, streaked down the slope of the desktop and slammed shut. Sam immediately tried to open it, but to no avail.

"I'm certain that can be fixed," he declared, pulling on the edge again. "In fact, I can fix that if you want, before you buy it."

Funny. I'd come to sell an ad but was now the prospect.

Then, all at once the top released from the base and Sam became obsessed with sliding the cover up and down, checking for glitches. He was so completely absorbed that I could have been juggling army tanks and he wouldn't have noticed.

I quickly decided to make my pitch and scoot along before things grew stranger.

"Actually," I began, "I wanted to see if you'd be interested in increasing your sales by advertising in *The Review*. I know you're familiar with the publication and our market."

Sam suddenly stopped fidgeting with the desk top. He looked directly at me, as if realizing my presence for the first time. In that split second his countenance darkened, feature by feature, as though an ominous cloud was passing over him.

"I thought you were here to do a follow-up piece on dioxin," he said and then quickly added, "I have no money in the ad budget." He sat down heavily in the desk chair. "Actually, I don't have an ad budget. I just can't advertise anywhere right now."

This was a standard line used to repel sales people. I'd heard it a thousand times. Yet, I sensed the genuineness of Sam's anguish.

"Well, then it's not the time to advertise," I encouraged, hoping to dislodge the cloud enshrouding him. "I imagine you do well with word-of-mouth and walk-in business."

"Are you moving?" I inquired, nodding towards the boxes, anxious to change the subject and leave.

To my surprise, the simple question released a tidal wave. In a few minutes I was awash in the flood waters of Sam Gafner's personal disaster: He and his wife, Brianna, had divorced four years ago. He was left with the flower shop he'd purchased and renovated for her. Only a few months after it opened Brianna developed a distaste for retail business and marriage. So she left the store and Sam. Unable to bear staying in the big house alone, Sam rented it to a friend and lived in the open warehouse space above the flower shop. All the money from his prestigious state job funded the unprofitable store. Then the friend moved out of the house, leaving him to manage two mortgage payments alone.

Why on earth was Sam Gafner telling me all this? Did I miss something in our exchange that would account for such candor? I wanted to quickly extract myself from this turbid swirl of unwarranted intimacy, so I finally said, "Somehow these things all work out for the best. I know you'll sell this desk too. It's beautiful."

I cleared my throat, nervously. "Well, thank you for your time. I appreciate it."

I began to leave but stopped and turned again to face Sam who was still watching me.

"By the way, I read the article in The Review about your solution to the dioxin issue. It is a brilliant idea. I hope it's well-received."

With that, I headed for the stairs again.

"What does your smallest ad cost?" he called after me.

I stopped and turned around for the second time, taken completely by surprise at this sudden reversal.

"It's $150 for a quarter page for one time. Or $400 if you buy three and pay in advance. But…"

Sam interrupted me before I could continue.

"Go ahead and schedule us for three times. Tell Alice downstairs I said it's o.k."

With that, Sam rolled himself in his one-hundred-year-old swivel chair to sit at the one-hundred-year-old desk and began scribbling again, seeming as old as his furniture.

Baffled, I managed a 'thank you', knowing the walls had a better chance of hearing than Sam did. He was absorbed once more and apparently had lost all auditory function. Handsome as he was, I hoped never to see the man again. He was a bit too erratic for my liking. Then again, I also hoped I might see him, which posed a problem since I happened to be married.

## Chapter 3

**That evening I excitedly told my husband**, Kurt, about meeting Sam The Great and selling three ads. Not surprisingly, he was indifferent. From my perspective indifference was Kurt Gustav's standard reaction to all things. Nevertheless, I insisted there was something cosmic involved. Kurt was quick to point out, however, that I thought this about *everything*. His 'so-what' response caused me to rethink. Perhaps Sam Gafner's life was just so big that everyone was bound to bump into it at some point, given the small confines of Jefferson City. Seeing him and finally selling three ads was just a predictable mathematical probability. That's all. Kurt was right to be unruffled. I'd finally sold some

ads to a big shot. That was that.

Evidently finished with our conversation, Kurt flipped

on the television, and I left to teach aerobics at the

studio downtown. I taught most weeknights after

working at The Review under the guise of earning extra

money. In reality, however, I wanted to avoid Kurt. I

also truly loved teaching and was thrilled that in a short

time, the classes had filled with a core group of women

who became regulars. Although it was a co-ed class, no

males ever attended, so we enjoyed a happy sisterhood

for an hour every evening.

As was my custom, I arrived early to prepare the

music. Soon the women began filling the room with

chatter and laughter. I noticed, however, that the

banter seemed much louder than usual. An odd

tension charged the atmosphere. As I turned from the

stereo to greet everyone, I instantly spotted two

dark-haired male heads at the back of the crowd. I

wasn't wearing my contact lenses so I couldn't see

details, but the men were nevertheless conspicuous, like

crows in a cornfield. The infiltrators had caused the

ladies to become an innervated pack of curious females.

I was equally curious, but their bold disruption also

irritated me.

As usual, I began warming up, then gradually picked

up the pace. As the music crescendoed, the two men

began making loud comments and exaggerated

movements. The pack giggled and the crows,

enormously flattered, continued adding more extravagance to their repertoire. I flashed friendly smiles of good humor but purposely stepped up the routine several notches to take the irksome crows out.

When class was over, I stayed in the front of the room to rewind the tapes for the next instructor. As I squatted to eject the cassette from the tape deck on the floor, I felt a presence. I looked sideways to see a pair of bare feet—a man's bare feet. Good Lord! I thought in panic. It's one of the crows! My eyes slowly climbed the subsequent body parts which led upward to a face. To my utter astonishment, it was the face of Sam Gafner!

The mouth on his face said, "Are you a dancer?"

The onslaught of thoughts bombarding my mind seemed to take several minutes:

*Is he serious?* I wondered at first…

Then,

*I've always wanted to be a dancer.*

Next,

*What a stupid line! But my goodness, his legs are as amazing as his face!*

And finally,

*I really can't stand this man.*

Thankfully, I managed to laugh and answered, "No. I don't dance. But thanks for asking. Maybe there's hope."

Then I quickly returned to ejecting the cassette tape.

"Well, you move like a dancer," Sam said, just like that.

*Well you move like a snake in the grass*, I thought to myself.

Embarrassed by the attention, I just smiled and began gathering my things from the floor. Then I rose and found myself standing face to face with Sam. Instantly, I realized I had just entered into a magnetically-charged vortex.

Sam and I stared at each other in awe. We were two virtual strangers, stunned by the force of our alarming similarities: the same dark hair, the same grey-blue eyes, two long, lanky frames. It was truly uncanny. But there was something else. Something invisible yet undeniably disconcerting despite Sam Gafner's pleasing exterior. Exactly what it was, I did not know, but it unnerved me. In my mind's eye, I detected a dark shadowy thing darting around him. Warning signals shot throughout my being.

"Well," I said, purposely breaking the spell, "I'd better go."

"Yes, I need to head out too," Sam mimicked. "Can I walk with you?"

I suppressed an urge to tear out of my skin and flee. Why did Sam Gafner want to walk me outside? Did he even remember meeting me at his flower shop? I desperately wanted him to go away but also wanted him to go with me. Spinning in paradox, I automatically lunged for my security net: journalistic interrogation.

"So, is dioxin really as toxic as they claim?" I blurted out.

Sam didn't pause for one millisecond at the ridiculous

randomness of the question. He skillfully flowed with it.

"Well, there's a huge controversy, but the reality is

that in high concentrations it's one of the most toxic

chemicals around. However, at Times Beach it had

been diluted to a concentration of 300 parts per

billion."

As Sam continued talking, relief swept over me.

Toxic soil was much safer than walking out the door

together. Buoyed by the safety net I knew so well, I

closed the conversation with the appropriate

professional comments, and Sam Gafner and I parted

company.

*You know you are still married*, I hissed accusingly to

myself as I walked to my car.

*I only spoke fifty words to the man!* I defended. *And by the way, I'm going home. I don't care how famous he is, or how handsome, I'm done with all this!*

And for forty-eight hours it was true.

But that Saturday, as I was trying on a dress in a store downtown, I heard two women in the next dressing room gossiping about Sam Gafner. By now I was not surprised at hearing The Name. One woman was speaking as if she was his girlfriend: "And he also has an undergraduate degree in physics." She went on but that was all I heard, as the word 'physics' thundered over and over in my ears. If Sam Gafner did not have my attention before, he certainly did now.

For the past two years after teaching aerobics, I went to the public library to read *Scientific American* and

*Science Digest* before going home.  I was obsessed with anything relating to science, but I was particularly interested in physics:  The laws of Thermodynamics, the Doppler effect, time, black holes, the chaos effect, etc. My friends and family dismissed this interest as endearingly odd, so there was no one with whom I could discuss these things.

Having a degree in English and a white-knuckle fear of higher math, I was surprised at this incongruent interest. It was so compelling, however, that I longed to leave public relations and journalism to pursue another degree—in the sciences—maybe even health care since I was also intrigued with the human body.  However, the expense and logistics intimidated, so, a first step would be to just talk with someone knowledgeable.

Now, at last, here was a person with answers—and a degree in Physics of all things! If Sam Gafner knew about black holes and subatomic particles, I was going to extract every speck of information from his brain. All my negative impressions and trepidation regarding him vanished. Now Sam was elevated to a highly profitable site for an archeological dig: I would divide his brain into quadrants, pick assiduously through every particle for answers and relentlessly unearth mysteries.

I couldn't wait to see him again. I sensed he would return to my aerobics class with his sidekick. What male wouldn't revisit a roomful of women hopping around in leotards? And so it was, as sure as dogs return to their buried bones, Sam and his cohort appeared again the next evening.

When class ended, I quickly weaved through the crowded reception area searching for Sam's tall frame and distinctive dark wavy hair. Finally, I spied him holding court with a group of admiring, posturing females. They had backed him into the groping leaves of a giant banana plant. I persistently edged my way through the half-circle of women. Normally I would have walked clear around such a throng to avoid contact of any sort. But not now. I was on a mission.

"I'm so sorry to interrupt, but I have to ask you a quick question—is it true you have a degree in physics?" I fired point blank while my heart thrust itself wildly against my ribs.

The bevy of women, irritated at my upstaging, repositioned themselves around him, edging me out, ever so slightly.

"Actually, I do. Why do you ask?" Sam answered, obviously curious.

As if performing water ballet, the women all turned their heads in unison to stare at me. Though I was not nearly as attractive as any of them, I had nevertheless won Sam's attention. The women looked peeved and baffled.

"So, you know all about absolute zero and black holes?" I persisted.

"Well, yes. I do." Sam answered, his cautious response pregnant with questions.

"Jackpot!" I yelled, slapping my leg in triumph.

At this, the bevy of women, obviously derailed, began

dispersing in defeat and Sam and I walked out together,

gripped in conversation.

Oddly, however, during the first half hour of our

exchange, I noticed that somehow, with each question I

asked about physics, Sam answered with a story about

himself. Amazingly, just as gravity wrestles all objects

into submission, Sam forced every new topic to spin

around himself. Like gravity, he was impressive and to

be respected. And just like gravity, he was rather

uninterested in anyone he attracted. Yet every time I

grew frustrated at being a living prop in his one-man

show, he artfully doled out just enough enticing

information to keep me in his orbit. I never even

realized I was being manipulated. Thus, I walked with

and listened to Sam Gafner for two full hours, feeling invisible and unimportant but hopeful and triumphant nevertheless. And before I knew it, this one-way exchange quickly became a pattern and continued for months, despite my constant unease and inner warnings to stop.

Then, one morning, out of the clear blue, Kurt announced that he wanted to try my aerobics class. His statement slashed the tightly-woven fabric of my private life and my instant resentment clearly signaled that our toothpick-structure marriage was about to collapse. Kurt was not welcomed in my world, but now he was particularly unwelcome because of Sam. Once again, however, I discounted my feelings as absurd and told myself that Sam was nothing more than a resource, like a great reference book at the library. No harm in introducing Kurt to a book.

A few evenings later, Kurt came to class and per the usual, Sam was there, waiting. He seemed to take Kurt's presence in stride, greeting us both very naturally. I followed suit and calmly introduced the one to the other as if it were the most natural thing in the world. But midway through, my nerves started snapping like firecrackers and my hands began to tremble. Fortunately, before I registered on the Richter scale, Sam tried to sell Kurt his home. Caesar's ghost! I thought, taken aback. The man certainly has a penchant along this line! I stood amazed listening to the sales spiel, only to witness Kurt agreeing to meet Sam at the house for a tour!

As I led class that night, I felt my life was a bizarre dream: there was Kurt awkwardly hopping around on one side of the room and the King of Everything doing each move perfectly on the other side. Needless to say, I didn't talk with Sam after class, nor did I see him the rest of the week. He was out of town on state business and I was grateful for the forced hiatus.

That Saturday morning, however, per the men's plan, Kurt and I arrived at Sam's house. As we walked to the porch, Sam eagerly came out to meet us. After the obligatory pleasantries, he began explaining every detail about the house to Kurt. This allowed me the freedom to wander around the near-empty home alone, gathering volumes of insight into the psychology of Sam Gafner.

The old house had much character but needed major renovation. Beyond the physical, it seemed like great sadness divided into sparsely furnished rooms. The pervasive heaviness made me very uneasy, so I was relieved when Kurt and Sam finally finished the tour. As we walked to the front door, I noticed a painting on one wall and stopped to look at the oil rendering of an old man. His face was long and forlorn, and his hair was thick and unkempt—not from being too busy to care, but too depressed for personal hygiene. Two haunting eyes stared bitterly at his vanished youth somewhere beyond the canvas. One might have thought at first glance that the old man looked exceedingly wise from many years and seasons of life.

But on closer examination, he was actually a middle-aged man grown old too soon.

As I gazed at the portrait, I was shocked to realize I was looking at Sam—his future self—perhaps thirty years or so down the road! My reaction further shocked me: I wanted to rip it off the wall before it came to pass. Kurt and Sam stopped talking and stood with me. We all looked at the painting.

"You like it?" Sam queried rhetorically. "An old friend of mine painted it years ago when we were in our early twenties. It's a study in black, white, and grey. She said it was me. Makes me look really wise and noble, huh?" He laughed, feigning modesty.

My thoughts screamed, *Is the man BLIND? This portrait is a blooming death warrant!*

"It's so. . . monochromatic." I lamely replied, hoping

to hide my concern.

We continued making our way to the front door,

discussing the house all the while. As we thanked Sam

for the tour, Kurt told him he would think about buying

the house. Then Kurt added, "So, Effie and I will pick

you up tonight around 7:00, right?"

"That's great," Sam replied. "Cindy and I will be

ready,"

In the car, as we pulled away from the curb, I turned

to Kurt and shrieked, "WHAT?"

"We're just going to dinner Effie," he stiffly replied.

"No need to shriek."

He calmly continued, "Sam told me to pick the

restaurant,"

Instantly, I cringed. Not another grueling night at Das Stein Haus!

It was the only German restaurant in town and no matter the occasion, we were there. It could be Diwali in India or Rosh Hashanah somewhere and we were at Das Stein Haus. Because Kurt was German. So very German.

"I'm thinking we'll go to Das Stein Haus," Kurt mused out loud, as though it were a thought nouveau.

"What a surprise!" I enthused sarcastically. "Another chance to wear my lederhosen and wolf down meat!" Kurt stared straight ahead, but I saw him roll his Gustav eyes. Ignoring me, he nonchalantly explained how Sam had invited us to 'double date'—that's the word he actually used. Double date. Evidently Sam had a grand time with Kurt on the tour and wanted to continue the

fun. Kurt acted as though this were as common as sand

on a beach. But I knew full well he was completely

shocked and deeply pleased to be rubbing elbows with

Sam Gafner.

Sam's date was Cindy Primm. All I knew about her

was that she worked in the governor's office. What on

earth would I talk to her about? What on earth would

we all talk about? Given my private talks with Sam, this

new turn of events really threw me for a loop.

"Did he really use the word 'double date?'" I asked

Kurt as we drove home.

"Yes!" Kurt retorted, clearly peeved. "What's the big

deal?"

"It's just such a 50's pep-squad thing to say," I answered. "Why on earth do you think he asked us to go out? We don't even know him." I paused for a split second and added, "Are you really serious about buying that depressing house?!"

"Effie. For God's sake," Kurt snapped. "You blow everything out of proportion! We're just having dinner with the man. People go out together. It's not a big deal." he said, abruptly ending the conversation.

Not surprisingly, the evening was wrought with strange contrasts. Cindy Primm looked like her name. She wore a blazer with shoulder pads and a matching skirt. Business attire. I wore jeans and a gauzy flowered top. When Cindy ordered 'the duck' for dinner I began to feel nauseated by memories of my pet duck, Amos

Millen, who took naps with me. When the waiter

presented Cindy's duck—dead, plucked bald, and

browned—I instinctively clutched Kurt's arm and

groaned heavily in his ear, "The agony! The agony!"

Sam, overhearing incorrectly exclaimed, "That was a

great movie! But I forget—who played Michelangelo?"

All the while, a heavy-set woman in a German barmaid

costume (one size too small) strolled among the tables

banging out German polkas on her accordion.

For a solid hour we shouted meaningless pleasantries

at one another, trying to be heard over other shouting

patrons and blasting polkas. When the torture finally

ceased, Sam invited us to his apartment for a glass of

wine. Not on your life, I thought. One can only take

so much, what with the duck, the polkas, and Kurt suddenly turned game show host.

But Kurt gleefully accepted the invitation. Gleeful and Kurt were not acquainted, but now, to my utter astonishment, Kurt wholeheartedly embraced a romping gleefulness regarding Sam Gafner. Such a spell-binder, that man.

Sam's loft looked amazing. The boxes were gone, and the expansive warehouse space invited us with open arms. A large, worn, oriental rug stretched across the old pine floors. Nestled in one corner was the roll-top desk and chair. In the opposite corner was a cozy armchair. A large, airy ficus tree arched over the right side of the chair and an old floor lamp stood guard on the left. In between the furniture, hanging on the exposed brick wall, was a huge brightly-colored abstract painting. On the other side of the room was a massive counter, which Sam had made to separate the kitchen from the sitting area.

He brought out some old wooden folding chairs and we sat in a circle on his rug, savoring the exquisite chocolate mousse he had made and chilled in paper cups. The warm yellow lamplight softened the room as well as our collective mood. After we finished the mousse, Sam poured us each a glass of Rothschild Lafite1979 and we began to feel bohemian and cool. While we were all conversing, Sam got up to locate a particular album and place it on his old stereo turntable. Suddenly a crackling sound filled the room, followed by a familiar, deeply resonate voice: "Early one morning,

Peter opened the gate and went out into the big green meadow." Then a great burst of violin music swept us into glorious optimism.

Spontaneously I jumped up and shouted, "Peter and the Wolf! I can't believe it! I haven't heard this in years! Can I see the album cover?"

Sam turned the sound down so we could all talk. Cindy and Kurt commented that they'd never heard of Peter and the Wolf and began to discuss music together. I went to the stereo to read the familiar description of how each animal in Prokofiev's children's story was represented by an instrument. United by the music, Sam and I eagerly waited for each sonic vignette. Sam's favorite was "Grandfather", represented by the bassoon. My favorite was the bird—a flute. Listening, I felt my childhood amalgamate with Sam in the present moment, completely separating us from Kurt and Cindy, who no longer seemed to exist.

Oh, the deep subtleties of togetherness and separateness—and the wiles thereof! And who on earth could fathom the power of a night with Sam Gafner and Peter and the Wolf?

Chapter 4

**Exit plans are basically all the same.** But I began mine
somewhat early—on my wedding day.

Anne Kincaid, my lifelong friend and maid of honor,
tried to talk me out of marrying Kurt on the way to the
church. Not the ideal conversation to have an hour
before the ceremony. It was shattering for her to
counter my plans at this inopportune juncture for many
reasons. But mainly, she had broken a sacred pact that
our group of seven girlfriends operated by: we never
questioned each other's decisions. To us, accountability
was invasive and confrontation, vulgar. We preferred
the crippling dysfunction of enablement. Yet in this

moment, how I wished one of them had confronted

me months ago.

"You don't have to do this Effie," Anne offered as I

parked the car in back of the church and turned the

ignition off. Her words were a scalpel, slicing through

layers of denial, exposing the unspoken. There it was,

laid wide open before us. Our eyes met and locked in

agreement: I was about to make a monumental

mistake. While I clearly saw the freedom I desperately

desired, I also knew I couldn't own up to it.

"It's too late," I answered, shifting my eyes downward.

"I can't humiliate Kurt and his family."

Anne looked away. "O.K." she acquiesced. "Then

I'm on board,"

Within an hour the vows were exchanged, the photographs taken, and for the next three years, I tried hard to be married—an impossible feat given my resolve to leave. Thus, I was the perfect image of a hypocrite: I wore my wedding ring, but secretly looked for apartments. I decorated our living room but purchased an old red Volkswagon to be my escape car. Then, I opened a checking account in my name and dreamed of being free. Surprisingly, Kurt seemed oblivious to my duplicity. Apparently as long as we spent every Sunday with his depressed parents and stopped on the way home to eat Peanut Buster Parfaits at Dairy Queen, he was content.

But three years, or one hundred and fifty-six parfaits later, I was done with my mega-caloric charade.

Further, divorce seemed to saturate the air like so much spring pollen: Dad had just left mom after 31 years of marriage, Anne was divorcing her husband and two more of our seven friends' marriages were in a death spiral, as was my brother's marriage. If I divorced Kurt now it would blend in nicely with the surrounding landscape. Two wrongs don't make things right, but many make one feel less wrong. Isn't that how the saying goes?

All this is to say that Sam was not my reason for wanting to divorce Kurt. But after that enchanted evening at his loft apartment, my long-incubated hope of leaving sprouted big fluffy wings, which I preened with great delight. Now it was just a matter of waiting for the right time to break the news.

In the meantime, my double-life with Sam continued.

Oddly, we never mentioned Kurt or of Cindy Primm.

Our sights were elevated to the mysteries of the uni-

verse. Sam began leaving me messages at work—

invitations to learn about the Karst topography of

Missouri limestone, or a session about crinoids and

brachiopods embedded in the Burlington Deposit. He

even arranged to have a guard take us outside the

dome of the state capital building one evening so I

could view the Mighty Missouri unobstructed. Sam

seemed elated with my insatiable interest in learning

and I loved his increasingly frequent 'information

invitations.'

And because he only talked about himself or about the

earth, there was no emotional bond between us really—or so I kept telling myself.

In addition to these private invitations, Sam also invited Kurt and me to the birthday party he was throwing for himself at a local tavern. Kurt, of course, was delighted. So we joined the celebration on a balmy night in July, thirty-six years after Sam Gafner's earthly debut. After a few drinks, Kurt joined a group of inebriated men in the corner who were passionately discussing St. Louis Cardinals baseball. This allowed me the freedom to meet many new, interesting people. My cheeks grew flush and my heart lifted higher with each enervating verbal exchange. After wrestling the theory of Absolute Zero with the inventor of a solar-powered outhouse, I turned to leave and ran smack-dab into the birthday boy.  He had been listening to the

conversation.

"Sam!" I yelled enthusiastically.  "Did you hear that

conversation?!"

"Absolutely!  And I have zero comments," he shot

back, grinning broadly at his own humor.

Then he pulled me closer to him and whispered, "I've

had three beers, so I could tell you I think you are

special.  I want you to know that."  Instantly, I felt I'd

been struck by lightning.  But to my surprise I calmly

said, "I know," and walked off like Scarlet O'Hara being

pithy with Rhett Butler.  However, in that brief second

of feigned composure, my heart had inconveniently

leapt into my pharynx making it difficult to breathe.  I

frantically rushed outside to demand its retreat in

private, only to have it tattle like a snit little sister:

*Sam Gafner likes you.*

*He likes a lot of girls!* I shot back.

*But you're the one he takes on outings most every*

*weeknight. You and Sam are falling in love,* it taunted.

*MAY DAY! MAY DAY!* I broadcasted frantically to my

entire self. But it was too late. I was already fixated on

being in love. It was so strong and captivating that I

didn't even realize my motive for divorcing Kurt had

suddenly mutated—from a guppy to a toad.

No matter. I witlessly leapt off the forbidden cliff

anyway—for a man I barely knew, before I was even

divorced, because he thought I was special. Brilliant.

In my delusion, I was convinced this was the

opportunity I'd been waiting for. And so that night

after Kurt went to bed, I crept into my office in our

second bedroom to write a poem. A goodbye poem.

I thought a poem seemed less cruel than just telling

Kurt point blank that I wanted a divorce. This was the

way of the English major (or a self-absorbed coward)

and it went like this:

## Sighs or Tears

Is it better not to say goodbye

And leave the leaving unannounced,

To let goodbye evaporate

Like dew becoming air?


Should goodbye fade like dusk to night

And shadow once familiar forms

'Til stars, like bits of shattered glass,

Reflect life parts of yesterday?


Silent, Summer slips to Fall

As verdure turns to earthen hue,

Yet not 'til wet leaves paint the ground

Is it noticed, Summer's gone.


When I finished the poem, I wept. When Kurt read

the poem, he didn't cry or try to persuade me to stay.

When I said I wanted a divorce, he simply got up from the couch, ran his fist through the door of our antique pie safe, and left. Several discussions followed once he came home, but within three months, our marriage of three years was over—a heartless ratio. Worse, from that standpoint, I found an apartment just one week after my announcement and moved immediately. Who was it who said, "A life unexamined is no life at all?" I think it was Socrates and I fancy that he was prophetically describing my life. Well, maybe not. Regardless, it never occurred to me to examine my behavior or the consequences of my actions. And I certainly didn't consider how I was affecting Kurt. Oh, I tried to appear considerate by giving him everything, including my wedding ring. But all I cared

about was being free.

And so, free I was. Me, myself, and I. All free, and

unexamined.

Chapter 5


**Getting what you want can be terrifying**—at least it

was for me. So, to abate my fear I became radically

social: gadding about with a large group of divorcees

and singles. To cope with our individual and collective

restlessness, we gathered at a local bar after work and

on weekend nights to drink our drinks and talk fervently

about life into the wee hours. We believed our

pontifications and aimless lives bore import because we

read the *New Yorker* and listened to NPR.

It was in this context that I encountered a part of

myself I never knew existed and was shocked to meet.

For instance, when Sam was asked to speak at a

conference in Italy in October, I thought it would be fun

to just fly over one day and meet him for lunch. I'd spent a summer in Europe and surmised that some of my molecules must still be there. Why not join them and Sam? Never mind that I was not yet officially divorced or couldn't afford to pay my parking tickets, let alone buy a round-trip plane ticket.

When Sam realized I was truly serious he told me he was confused about my intentions and called for a lunch meeting at a local Mexican restaurant. As we ate our enchiladas, I assured him I merely thought lunch in Europe would be fun and make a great story. To compound that absurdity, Sam happened to mention that his old girlfriend, Heather, had just moved in with him—because her house had burned to the ground with her Labrador retriever in it! WHAT!!??

Given all Sam's overtures towards me, I was crushed by this news...even though I had no hold on him. However, I couldn't express my hurt given the poor girl's horrific situation. Who complains about someone whose house and dog are rendered to charcoal? So instead of being honest and protecting myself, I offered concern and never addressed the disheartening fact that Sam was living with this girl yet considering a rendezvous in Europe with me. But then again, I was the one who was married, wasn't I? Hmmm. Thus, with no moral leg to stand on, I foolishly feigned being care-free and woundless. At any rate, by the time the waitress brought our checks, Sam had eagerly taken to the idea. I then proceeded to make it happen, against all odds.

This required lying to a lot of people, working until midnight for two weeks straight, charging $800 on my visa card (which I had no way of paying), and finally rocketing past traffic jams and dodging highway barricades to reach the airport in St. Louis on time. Sam lied to his co-workers about needing to leave early after his presentations and met me at the airport in Luxembourg. We laughed, had lunch, and rode on a hydrofoil boat down the Rhine to look at castles. Then on a whim we caught the Eurail train to Paris and ate dinner at a charming café. It was there that we decided to part company. I don't remember what prompted such a conversation, but we conceded that since I wasn't divorced and Sam was living with the fragile

Heather, we were on a bad tangent and should stop seeing each other.

There we sat with our conclusion at a small bistro table, pushed against a window. On the other side of our reflection, the rainy Parisian night seemed to go on forever. As I watched the raindrops pelt the image of my face and drench my soul, the low-grade depression I'd been dodging most of my life hit me like an eighteen-wheeler. I had hoped Sam would say he wanted us to be together. Yet, instead of being candid, I went chin-up and cheery like always.

The next morning I even helped Sam pick out a scarf for Heather to prove I was fine. Just fine. Then we took a train to Luxembourg to fly back to Missouri and go our separate ways. But at that café in Paris I had changed. My heart was tired of aching. And I noticed

for the first time that my unexamined life had a nasty

habit of ruining things. Nevertheless, I was helpless to

change.

Back home, my friends reveled in the story, which

only fueled my growing penchant for exploits. And as it

happened, an opportunity for another adventure

surfaced—at a party one night. A new friend and I

were talking about how we'd never seen our livers,

lungs, hearts, kidneys, etc. We thought it unreasonable

that they do so much for us yet remain unobserved.

Another friend was listening to the conversation and

straight away lead Harriet and I through the crowd to

introduce us to his doctor friend who was a pathologist

at the local hospital. On hearing our complaint, he invited us to observe an autopsy.

Well, we couldn't believe our good fortune, so I gave him my work number to call when he had a body. The plan, hatched after a beer or two, seemed exceedingly grand and Harriet and I agreed to go together no matter what. Two months passed and we had completely forgotten our agreement but one afternoon at work, I received a call from the hospital. They had a body prepared for an autopsy and were alerting me to come at four o'clock that afternoon. I thanked the lady—an odd thing given the subject matter—and I told her I'd be there. Horrified at what I'd just done, I immediately called Harriet so she could arrange to go with me.

"No way!" She shrieked. "I wasn't really serious Effie! Were you?"

I had to stop and think before answering. "I never thought I'd get a call, but I told the doctor I'd come. I have to do it."

"Wait," Harriet said. "Let me get this straight. You ditch your husband who you never wanted to marry, run off to Europe with Sam Gafner before you're divorced, lie to your boss about where you were, and now you're all noble about keeping some drunken dare?"

"I'm not noble. I'm just curious. I want to see what organs look like. And I need to know if I can handle that kind of thing—in case this is a new career path."

"You told me you throw up when you get a shot!"

Harriet exclaimed. "This is not a needle stick in your

arm, Effie! Its's a saw cutting through a dead person's

entire sternum, for God's sake!"

"Harriet! Stop! This could inspire me to get a degree

in biology!" I repeated, trying hard to deflect her

convincing arguments. "It's such a rare opportunity!

You've got to come with me and learn something new.

We can't just sit in offices our whole lives, Harriet! Fear

dry rot of the soul! Come with me!"

"Oh, my God!" she exclaimed, "You are nuts! There

is no way I'm going. I hate blood, men in lab coats, and

dead bodies. Call me as soon as you're done."

Harriet hung up the phone and I realized I was in this

crazy thing alone. But I recalled what a friend of mine

always said after reciting Gunga Din: "Knees up. Head down. Drive through." The image of navigating in fetal position perplexed but nevertheless motivated somehow—so I gathered my things and with newfound pluck, headed for the car.

At the hospital, an orderly led me to the room with the body and told me the doctor would be coming soon. When he left, I nervously turned to look at the cadaver on the stainless steel lab table. There, rigid like a fallen statue, was an old man. Oddly enough, he was wearing a pin-striped dress shirt. That was all. Autopsy attire? His thin transparent skin was the color of under-cooked egg whites. This was all shocking enough but his face—bone structure, nose, and all—looked just like my father!

I blinked my eyes in disbelief thinking I was just imagining the resemblance. On further observation, I realized he was much shorter and much older than Dad—and of course dead, but other than that, the likeness was alarming. Trying to calm down, I looked around the room for a visual diversion. I was relieved to see some shelves along one wall. They were lined with labeled jars filled with clear liquid and strange things that appeared to be organs.

Curious, I walked over for a closer look and saw that one of the jars held the kidney of George Goetz, my childhood neighbor. He had been a prominent attorney and last I saw him, he was whole. Seeing his lonesome kidney floating in a jar compounded my distress and I suddenly realized with all certainty that health science was not the next career path for me.

My happy, hard-won epiphany was rudely interrupted

as the pathologist burst in the room, obviously in a

great rush.

"Are you ready Ms. Millen?" he demanded. "I need

to speed this up! Glad you could make it," he declared,

with no mention at all of our previous inebriated

agreement. "Here, you have to wear these." He

barked, handing me a lab coat and safety glasses. Then

he pulled a circular saw from a cabinet and laid it on the

counter.

At that point, I found myself pointing feebly and

muttering, "My neighbor's kidney is on that shelf and

this man looks just like my father."

Oblivious to my pitiful dribble, the doctor looked at the corpse and immediately yelled to the orderly in the outer room. "Why is this man in a shirt! And where is his toe tag and paperwork for crying out loud!?" His face reddened with anger. "This is unacceptable! "I can't even start!" The orderly apologized and dashed off to search for the missing items. The doctor grabbed some latex gloves, and a pair of scissors. He handed them to me and said, "Here, put these on. You can cut this shirt off."

My knees suddenly became warmed marshmallows and my legs, limp larva. I feared I might collapse. "I've never touched a dead person," I stammered, my voice quivering uncontrollably.

"For crying out loud!" he shouted. "I let an ignoramus in here! Give me those scissors! I'll do it, for Pete's sake!" With that he grabbed the scissors and began cutting the shirt. He pulled the back section from the man and handed it to me. "What's that on the inside of the collar? It looks like a name—probably from the nursing home laundry. He kept cutting and asked impetuously, "So what's the name?"

If things weren't already surreal, they were now. The name, handwritten in bold, permanent black marker, was M-I-L-L-E-N. My head began to swim, yet somehow I managed to speak my last name.

"Wait! That's your name!" The doctor exclaimed. "He stopped cutting and looked bug-eyed at me. "Do you know this guy?"

"No." I said. "But he looks just like my dad. He can't

be a relative though—we are the only Millens in town."

Just then the orderly rushed in with the toe tag and

papers. The doctor flipped through the documents and

said, "His name is Jim Millen from Joplin, Missouri."

"Unbelievable!" I exclaimed. "My father grew up

about 15 miles from Joplin! I looked again at the

familiar face. "He really could be a relative!"

The doctor had already refocused on the job at hand

and was unresponsive to my musings. He quickly

proceeded with the autopsy and discovered that Jim

Millen had died of pleurisy. The doctor completed all

the forms and closed the case, but I couldn't.

For several weeks after the autopsy, I tried finding out

more about Jim Millen, all to no avail. The only thing I

discovered was that he was a truck driver, spending his last days in town with his married daughter whose last name was Evans. She was understandably resistant to talking with me, so I abandoned my search. But I couldn't abandon the certainty that something was trying to tell me something: for a few horrifying minutes I feared a cosmic directive to drive trucks. Then I spent two days worried that the dead look-a-like was an omen of my father's untimely death.

When that dissipated, I began to think it was simply a sign that science was a 'dead end' pursuit for me. Deep down this seemed to ring true. Nevertheless, the whole thing remained a haunting mystery—a humorous thing given that is was now Halloween. Trick or treat.

Chapter 6

**Our group of friends had decided to attend a**

**costume party** which was sponsored by the Downtown

Merchants' Association at the iconic Governor Hotel. I

came as Dylan Thomas and was having a high time in

my knickers and newsboy hat quoting, *Do Not Go Gentle*

*Into That Good Night,* until I ran into Sam and Heather

dressed as a pair of poker cards. Feeling trumped, as it

were, I nevertheless determined to enjoy the evening.

While dancing with a good friend who worked at *The*

*Review,* I noticed Sam making his way over to us. I

watched in amazement as he rudely cut in on Charlie.

Sam knew I was now divorced, but I'd neither seen

him nor heard from him since our return from Europe.

Despite the unaddressed disconnect, however, the next

thing I knew I was dancing with Sam Gafner. Song after

song we danced—like Yule Brynner and whats-her-

name in *The King and I*. We danced so long that Sam's

playing card poster fell off and I lost my newsboy hat.

After three hours, the band broke down their

equipment and we were forced to stop and actually

talk. Only then did Sam tell me Heather had moved

out and they were now just friends. "But you came as

matching cards," I pointed out. "That makes you a

pair," I said, smiling.

"Well you came as Dylan Thomas and you're not a

British male poet," Sam rebutted, pleased with his quick

comeback. "Besides, when you went to the restroom,

Heather came over to say she thinks you and I should be together. She could see it clearly. And I agree."

Well there it was, straight from the horse's mouth, so to speak. As Sam spoke, time slammed on the brakes, but my head crashed through the windshield. This talk of togetherness that I'd ached to hear in Paris was now scaring me.

*Effie! Effie Tennessee Millen! Can you hear me?* my *paramedic-self intervened. I don't care what he says, Sam ditched Heather to be with you in Paris and ditched YOU in Paris because of her. Plus, he knew you were divorced and never even called! And NOW Prince Charming shows up with her but ends up with you and they both think you should be together? HE IS DANGEROUS! I REPEAT! HE IS DANGEROUS! RUN!*

My sympathetic nervous system was definitely aroused but confused whether to fight or flee because all I wanted to do was faint (not one of Cannon's Stress Response options). Paralyzed by cerebral lockdown, my reptilian brain grabbed the wheel and I became a talking iguana,

"You what?" I asked slowly and hoarsely. And then, just like that, bold Sam Gafner kissed me and told me he was walking me home.

Both apartments in the two-story 1890's home were pitch dark. My neighbor who lived in the first floor was blind so he never used lights. His name was Albert and for some unknown reason, on the day I moved in, he assigned himself as my protector. He often waited up for me if I was out—swinging on the porch swing we

had jointly purchased. Like most blind people, Albert
could hear any slight sound. But regarding me, his
hearing was even more acute. Thus, as Sam and I came
closer, we saw Albert stop swinging and bend forward
to listen.

"Effie?" he called, looking straight out into the night as
if he could see me there. "Who's that with you?"

"Hi Albert," I answered as we walked closer. "It's a
friend of mine. Sam, this is Albert Gabriel. Albert this is
Sam Gafner."

"Uh-uh," Albert commented under his breath—but
just loud enough to be heard. "I see a jackal on
Halloween. And he ain't no treat. Girl, you in for
trouble!"

## Chapter 7

**A few days later, I found myself coming out of anesthesia** as a nurse helped me sit up.

"In all my years I've never seen anyone smiling after surgery! You've been grinning for thirty minutes!" she chortled, putting pillows behind my back.

I immediately noticed that my whole right hand was bandaged as a support for my little finger which had been splinted and taped separately. The very tip of the finger was exposed revealing a metal pin with a rubber band attached to it.

"Is this nail thing glued to my finger?" I asked, trying not to sound alarmed.

"Oh no, Honey. The doctor drilled a hole in the tip of the bone and screwed in the pin," the nurse replied. "It's for resistance exercises to keep the finger from curling up permanently as it heals."

With that, I promptly threw up all over myself. So much for the smiley recovery. Who would have guessed that a visit to Sam Gafner's apartment would land me in the hospital with a pin embedded in my pinky?

It started the day before when Sam asked me to come over. His plan was to go for a run together. It was Sunday, so the flower shop was closed. As I walked to the front door, Sam stuck his head out the window upstairs, "Effie! The door's open! Come up for a second." I found Sam lacing his new running shoes and we began talking about where to run. Suddenly, we heard someone coming in the shop downstairs.

"Shoot!" Sam exclaimed, "I should have told you to lock the door." Then he yelled, "Is someone there?"

"Hi! It's me! I'm coming up." We heard quick footsteps on the stairs and turned to see Heather bounding into the room. She stopped in shock to stare at us— staring in shock at her. Sam began stammering lame pleasantries and I nervously blurted out, "Wow! You can really fly upstairs! Well, I need to scoot."

Then, I darted down the steps to make myself invisible as quickly as possible. However, my effort to be unnoticed backfired as midway down, my foot slipped, causing me to fall. There was no drywall or railing so I frantically tried to grab the wall studs. My little finger caught on the raised metal corner of an exposed metal light switch plate and lodged there while I went on. Thankfully, however, I jarred to a halt on the step below. I pushed myself back up one stair to dislodge my finger and noticed blood pouring down my arm. At first glance, it appeared that the top third of my finger had been nearly severed.

On the verge of fainting, I was grateful that Sam was quickly at my side asking if I was OK. I kept telling him I was fine and just needed to go home. But he insisted on taking me to the emergency room—leaving Heather on her own. At the hospital, we learned the tendon and nerves in my finger were severed and the bone had been slightly cut. The next thing I knew, I was being rolled into surgery.

The following day, once I was back home, Sam told me that he had ended his 'friendship' with Heather— my injury being a catalyst somehow. Almost severing a finger didn't compare to a having a house burn down with your dog in it, but you play the cards you're dealt. And while I'd rather have won Sam's affections by beauty or talent or character, my disfiguring injury did prove that there are other ways to skin a cat— evidenced by the fact that Heather was a thing of the past.

Through that autumn, winter, and early spring Sam and I were inseparable. Every weeknight after work he came to my aerobic classes. Then we would jog a few miles and end up eating dinner at a favorite downtown restaurant. On weekend days we hiked or navigated the Missouri River in Sam's johnboat and at night we socialized at 'our tavern'.

Then one day, out of the blue, Sam's ex-wife called him. She was coming in town from Texas and wanted him to throw a party for her with all their old friends. He happily agreed to accommodate the request and invited me as his date. Though we were of the liberal woodstock generation, I was not liberal at heart, so the arrangement seemed wrong and hurtful. On the other hand, I certainly didn't want Sam to think I wasn't cool and open-minded like he and Brianna. My friends all thought I was stupid to go. But my fear of rejection made me chase after stupidity. Like a moth to flame.

Anne had met Brianna and knew a lot about her somehow. Everything she told me increased my dread:

Brianna was tan and beautiful and classy. She was from southern California and dressed accordingly. Her father was a prominent Doctor and her mother a southern belle sophisticate. They were divorced because he was an alcoholic. Brianna had been married before, but she divorced that husband also. She smoked pot and had hippy, avant-garde friends. Did I say she was tan and beautiful? That's what everyone seemed bent on telling me. Brianna was very tan and very beautiful. Sam said she had great legs and a temper. She had thrown her spaghetti and meatballs at him two nights before their wedding because he suggested she have her hair done locally. But she had great legs. And a great face. And she was tan and classy and beautiful (this is not a misprint repetition). And the rumor among the flower shop employees was that Sam still loved her.

Well, it appeared I'd jumped from the pan into the fire, as it were…with no flame retardant. Silly me. But I had a plan—a slingshot and a stone like David used to fell Goliath: I borrowed shorts and a top from a friend at work because my clothes weren't cool enough, and I couldn't afford to buy something new. As it turned out they were two sizes too big and I looked like the Liberty Bell—my legs and feet being the clapper. No matter. I had basked in the sun for three hours to be tan like Brianna. And I would have been if not for the severe sunburn down one side of my entire body which caused one eye to swell shut. Who knew a retaining wall was shading half my body? Not to worry. I had props: I brought my plastic horn-rimmed glasses with a giant plastic nose and a fake mustache—for comic relief if the need arose.

You may be wondering if Sam picked me up for the date. No he didn't. So I drove myself to the flower shop and walked in alone to meet the woman who still had his heart even though she'd been gone for four years.

"Effie! I can't believe you're here!" three friends shouted scurrying around me as I walked in the flower shop. One whispered, "She's here—upstairs—and Sam seems nervous. What on earth happened to your eye?"

My Pakistani friend, Raheem, who was also friends with Sam, saw me and kindly pulled me aside. He told me I looked great and that his five-year-old son Ahban, was upstairs and would love to see me. "He will make it easier for you to be up there with Brianna and Sam. Come on. I'll go with you." I was deeply grateful for the escort and very excited to see Ahban because we enjoyed a happy affinity for one another.

The stairs were dimly lit but I still noticed my blood stains on the two steps under the light switch. Raheem also noticed. "My God, that looks like dried blood!" Evidently Raheem hadn't heard about my accident.

"It is blood." I said knowingly. "It's mine. I fell and cut my finger trying to avoid Heather."

The whites of Raheem's eyes widened as he stopped to stare at me. "This man is not good for you, Effie! Why do you continue with him?" Our conversation was interrupted by people coming behind us and we all headed upstairs together.

It was so crowded in the loft that I didn't see Sam right away. This was fine with me as my intent was to simply enjoy people and let the chips fall where they may. Ahban saw me and came running over to give me a big hug. "Effette! Effette! You have come here!" he enthused in his sweet accent. I scooped him up in my arms and swung him around, then set him back down and said,

"Cover your eyes. I have a surprise for you." He obeyed and I turned my back to put on the plastic nose and glasses. "OK, count to three and uncover your eyes." As Ahban yelled 'three', I spun around to surprise him only to stand face to face with Brianna.

There she stood, all tan and beautiful and classy, staring at me. She wore a casual linen jacket with the sleeves pushed up and a classic long black tank dress. Her sun-streaked hair was perfect, her pure silver earrings and bracelet and simple necklace were perfect. Even her tan feet with one silver toe-ring were perfect. And there I was, a half-sunburned cyclops shaped like a clownish bell in my borrowed clothes and plastic nose.

There was a terrible split-second of shock as we noted our stark differences. At first glance, it appeared we only had three things in common: We were female bipeds, both breathed oxygen, and we shared Sam Gafner as our lowest common denominator.

Thankfully, in an act of mercy, Raheem interjected and introduced me as Sam's date, then took Ahban to get a drink of water.

"So you are Effie!" Brianna exclaimed. "Are those Ray-Bans?" she asked, pointing to my glasses. We laughed and then she immediately began talking about Sam. She told me when she met Sam he wore dingy turtle neck shirts and baggy Levi's so she had to teach him how to dress. She also repeatedly mentioned that he picked his cuticles incessantly which drove her crazy. As she talked I witlessly downed three glasses of wine—two past my limit. This calmed my jangled nerves so completely that the next thing I knew Brianna was gone and I was deeply engrossed in other fascinating conversations.

Despite my sloshy condition, I began to notice that the party was morphing from harmless gaiety to emotional free-for-alls. At one point, I found myself consoling a weeping young woman who was broken-hearted over her boyfriend leaving her. Oddly, in the middle of her lament, it suddenly occurred to me that two hours had passed and Sam hadn't even spoken to me. My anger grew as I pieced things together: I remembered spotting him earlier in the evening across the crowded room and he'd blown me a kiss. Then sometime after that I noticed him pontificating with groups of people here and there, but now he was nowhere to be seen.

I began looking downstairs in the shop for him, but he wasn't there. I looked outside, then back upstairs. No

Sam. Funny how sometimes you just know things.

Well, I knew Sam was with Brianna somewhere, and it

broke my heart. All I wanted to do was leave, so I

headed home on foot—completely forgetting my car.

Somehow along the way, however, I managed a detour

to the State Capital grounds where I crawled over a

massive concrete retaining wall on the river bluff. On

the other side, I slumped down against the wall grateful

for a private spot to sit and proceeded to cry my eyes

out.

The next thing I knew, there was a spotlight shining

on my head and a man in a uniform was asking if I was

OK. Even in my stupor, I was shocked and humiliated.

Three glasses of wine couldn't hide the realization that

I'd crossed an invisible line when I climbed over that

wall. *Effie Millen! WHAT are you doing!* my conscience

scolded. *Have you completely lost your scruples!?!*

"Sir," I gushed. "I've lost my scruples. Please go and

let me grieve these wounds inflicted by a callous, jackal

of a man."

"I'm sorry young lady. Really, I am. But I can't let you

stay here. You'll have to grieve on this side of the wall.

I can't have you falling off the bluff and hurting yourself."

He held out his hand to help me up.

"Blind Albert warned me. He told me to run." I

drunkenly informed the officer as he helped me over

the massive structure. "But I didn't listen."

"Can I tell you something young lady?" the officer

asked as I brushed dirt off my shirt. "Any man who

would make a nice girl like you crawl over a wall and

cry like this, can't be good for you. I agree with the blind guy—keep away from this fella. You're too good for him."

All I could do was sniffle and nod my head.

"Can you make it home now?" He asked kindly.

"Oh yes, sir. I just live a block east," I slurred, pointing west. "Thank you."

The officer left, but I noticed him looking back now and then to make sure I was really leaving. As I aimlessly approached my apartment building, I spotted Sam's florist van parked in front. Sam was in the driver's seat and jumped out when he saw me.

"Effie! I've been looking all over for you! Why did you just leave?"

"You need to go away," I gushed. "I know you were with Brianna."

Sam instantly looked guilty.

"I just kissed her a few times," he confessed. "She wanted to talk in private so we went to the basement for a while. We just talked and then I kissed her."

Sam and I had been routinely intimate so this news leveled me. I felt instantly weak and nauseated. Sam said he was sorry. But that didn't stop the pain...or repair the damage. And although we made up, a deep sense of worthlessness began a covert operation in my system. It excused Sam's actions and blamed me for not being attractive enough. The worthlessness prevented me from severing relations with this man who kept hurting me. It ushered me into the world of 'if only.' If only I were...Tan. Beautiful. Classy. Petite. Well-dressed. Always happy with no problems. Funnier. Smarter. Better educated. Wittier. If I could just have perfect hair and teeth and skin and a perfect body. If I could just not look like or be like me. That's what I needed. To not be me. Then Sam might not have kissed Brat—I mean Brianna.

In reality, however, what I really needed was outside intervention.

Chapter 8


**I didn't often see Dad since he divorced Mom.** He

was busy with his new wife, her younger children, and

work. So, when he called and asked to meet for lunch I

was excited. After catching up with each other's lives,

he pulled a brochure from his jacket pocket and handed

it to me.

"I know this sounds crazy, but when I saw this, I

thought you might be interested." His bright blue eyes

twinkled with expectation. "See what you think."

It was information on New York University's Book

and Magazine Publishing Summer Institute. As I read

about the program I felt I was coming alive. I knew I

had to go. However, there were many challenging

obstacles to hurdle.  And even if I managed to jump them all, I had no idea where I would land, what the purpose was, and how I would pay for it.  Nevertheless, I mustered the courage to proceed despite the fear of all the unknowns.

The essay and application deadline were in one week. And only 40 applicants would be accepted.  As I delivered my completed packet to the Post Office, I was ecstatic at the possible opportunity—yet equally fearful of being rejected and having to tell people I failed. Thus, I told no one what I was doing.  Within a week, I received a letter stating that my paperwork had been received along with nearly 2000 other applicants' submissions.  The letter also explained that the accepted forty would be determined sometime within the month.  So, for the next twenty-nine days I checked

my mailbox for a response.  Nothing.  On day thirty

when I looked yet again, I saw a large NYU envelope.

My heart pounded as I opened it and read the cover

letter:

Dear Ms. Millen,

Congratulations! On behalf of the admissions committee, I'm pleased to inform you that you have been accepted into the New York University's 1985 Summer Institute in Book and Magazine Publishing. The program this year will be the most thorough and exciting in the history of the Institute. It is our consensus that you will be an outstanding member of this year's select group of participants.

Information on the next steps is enclosed in this packet. Please read everything carefully and respond promptly with your payment and dormitory application. You will be receiving advance assignments in the next few days.

Congratulations again. We look forward to meeting you and helping you attain a career in publishing.

Sincerely,

Alan Simon

Director of Admissions

I climbed the stairs to my apartment, dropped

everything except the letter and sat at the top of the

steps, reading it over and over.  I was really going to

New York!  I threw the letter in the air and began

running around the apartment yelling to the walls that I

was going to New York.  Then I sat down and made a

list of all I had to do:

-secure a student loan

-give notice at work and leave everything in order

-terminate my apartment lease

-sell everything

-buy a one-way plane ticket to New York

-purchase a typewriter and ship it to the dorm

-set up a bank account in New York

-complete and submit all the assignments

-arrange for someone to keep my Volkswagon

-tell Sam

All this had to be done by June 10th. It was now early May, so I didn't have a lot of time.

Meanwhile, Sam had invited me to the Governor's Spring Open House. I was so excited to have a real date that I splurged and bought a dress. I also decided it would be the perfect time to tell Sam about New York. Magically, the new dress made me radiant and my little secret, mysterious...so when Sam appeared to escort me to the gala, there I was—glowing like Cinderella in her magic-wand taffeta—smirking like Mona Lisa.

The 1890's mansion was just a few blocks from my apartment, so we strolled there hand-in-hand, intoxicated by the sweet smell of the spring night air. As we approached the stately home, we instinctively stopped and stood in awe: Light cascaded from the elegant windows, skipping among shadowy oaks and lacy wrought-iron balustrades. Waiting on the grand front porch, was a gracious butler ushering us into a palace of light; crystal wine glasses shimmered on silver trays, tables draped in iridescent linens held endless sparkling punch bowls, gleaming platters laden with dazzling culinary delights bedecked every table, and massive mirrors reflected sparkling chandeliers, while soft spotlights highlighted grand paintings resplendent with stories of Missouri's rich heritage.

Waiters in radiantly white shirts and black bow ties smiled brightly as they served the well-dressed people in confetti colors. The hum of conversation innervated everything. Sam introduced me to so many people that my mind became a blur of faces and names. The fact that Dad had founded and published the only private magazine about Missouri was of great interest—many of the guests knew him or knew of him. After a while, however, the perfunctory accolades and posturing grew tedious and I found myself talking to the servers in the back room. How lively they were, despite working all afternoon and serving all evening. I began carrying dirty dishes to the kitchen just to be with them because they reminded me of Dad's family—so unassuming and fun.

As it grew later, I went back out to find Sam. He was sitting alone at a table as most of the guests had left. We said our goodbyes and leisurely strolled back to my apartment. As our conversation about the enchanting evening subsided, I decided it was a perfect time to tell

Sam about New York. I had no idea how he would respond, but I certainly was not prepared for what followed.

"You're actually serious? You're just running off to New York?" Sam asked angrily. "And you're just now telling me?" He paused, looking fiercely at me. "How long have you known you were leaving?" Before I could answer he continued, "Don't you see you're just fooling yourself? You aren't interested in publishing! You're just running away because you don't like your life here. This New York thing is an escape, but you're too immature to admit it!"

Completely stunned, I simply sat down on a retaining wall at the edge of the sidewalk.

"I can't believe you are saying these things!" I said, looking incredulously at Sam's angry face.

I'd hoped for a more tender dialogue. One where Sam might actually tell me how much he cared for me—something I'd never heard him say. Instead, however, his vitriol inflamed the old, Sam-inflicted wounds. For a millisecond I considered pushing Sam aside and walking away forever. But I apologized instead.

In such moments, one really should back away from the proverbial tree to see the forest—or make that one stitch in time to save nine. But tidy cliché living was lost on me, so I persisted in ramming trees and wearing unraveled things...and kept living with Kill-Joy.

Ironically, a few days later, I found the poem I'd

written the night Sam kissed me the first time.  It fell

from an old journal as I was cleaning out a closet.

Oddly, at the time, I felt as if something was writing it to

me.  I was not really the author.  So strange.  And while

I was deeply curious as to the meaning, mostly I was

just aggravated as I read it again.  Why didn't I just bask

in first-kiss afterglow for God's sake?  Oh no! I had to

write some cryptic warning poem that I didn't even

understand.  Regardless of my irritation, I kept reading it

over and over:

## One Stone

In this world,

there is no cause without effect:

no stone cast deep into the waters

without ensuing, circling waves

which rock a struggling, upturned bug,

and force moonlight to stretch and bend

through undulating dark.


What harm—one stone

thrust through the depths?

Perhaps it's not so much the stone

as the mute attempt to stay afloat.

Was I the upturned struggling bug? And who or what was the darn stone? I was an English major and wrote the stupid thing—or at least was used to write it. Surely, I could decode the meaning! But no. I only knew I was being warned and it had something to do with Sam—like Blind Albert's warning, and that shadowy thing darting around Sam after aerobics class. One thing I was certain of, however: I was not giving any more attention to these persisting creepy things. I was way too busy being dysfunctional to add creepy to the mix.

In the meantime, the newly-elected Governor advised Sam that he would not be reappointed to his position. He graciously allowed Sam to publicly announce he was resigning instead of being terminated. In fear of financial collapse, Sam feverishly immersed himself in drumming up consulting work.

Similarly, I was overwhelmed with undoing my life in Jefferson City. Finally, only five days before leaving for New York, I had a sale and, in a few hours, sold everything I owned, except the clothes I was wearing, the items in my suitcase, two small George Caleb Bingham prints, and my eleven-year-old Volkswagon with a hole in the floorboard. This was my vast estate. Before locking up and taking my key to the landlord, I wandered around the empty rooms, looking out the windows, stopping to listen to the silence. In that moment, I realized I wasn't just leaving my hometown. I was leaving all I'd ever known. I was excited, afraid, and sad all at once. It was one thing to plan an adventure, but another thing altogether to stand at its border,

empty-handed, ready to cross, with no one but your

unreliable self as a companion.

Chapter 9


**Two days later, after a life-threatening taxi ride from**

**LaGuardia,** I wobbled into the lobby of Brittany Hall—

my new home for the next eight weeks. In all my

planning, it never occurred to me that I would be

entering a micro world of the newly post-pubescent. I

was suddenly Gulliver among the Lilliputians...An

eighteen-year-old checked me in. I know because I

asked. With youths yelling and running everywhere, I

felt like a neon sign spastically flashing my old age:

owned a house, hung wallpaper, worried about grub

worms in my lawn, DIVORCED.

That evening we began orientation and the next day

we embarked on a very challenging schedule of classes

and assignments. Disoriented by the overwhelming

newness of everything, I developed a routine in hopes

of feeling more secure. This consisted of:

-eating a blueberry bagel every morning

-talking to the beggars in Washington Square

on the way to class

-jogging around Greenwich Village

-grabbing dinner at D'Agostino's deli

-eating alone in my room

-studying

-standing in line at the lobby pay phones, hoping

to call home

-dropping in bed and sweating myself to sleep in the

suffocating heat

Despite my security-blanket routine, however, in just

five short days I'd been:

-approached by drug dealers repeatedly

-followed by a scary man who stopped only when

 I yelled that his mother would be ashamed of him

-addicted to arugula

-lost in the subways four times

-mistaken for Barbara Streisand by a drunk

-unable to keep up with Madonna during a

 90-minute aerobic class- yes, Madonna

-invited by a gentleman to live with him in Egypt

-interrogated by a Presbyterian

-told by an inebriated Kurt Vonnegut to scrap

 the first three chapters of any book I was writing

-knocked into a pile of trash


It occurred to me that like it or not, I was being

inexorably pressured into the Big Apple mold:

pressured by lack of space, pressured by constant

noise and movement, pressured to get somewhere,

pressured for time, pressured to compete for

everything— a place in line, a seat, a dollar, a chance.

I'd unwittingly joined the other wild-eyed salmon

writhing against the current. Welcome to New York.

I was too busy to think about Sam specifically. But

nevertheless, the man was generally always on my

mind…and the ache of him still fresh. However,

sometime in the midst of the second week, I noticed I

wasn't missing him as much. I even detected a tender

mending of wounds. So wouldn't you know when I

called Sam that night, he announced that his new client

needed him to be in New York. He was coming that

weekend and staying the week. I was so anxious to see

him—yet devastated to lose my new-found freedom. I

knew my heart wanted more time to really heal, but my

excitement won out and I invited Sam to come and stay with me.

The evening before he arrived, I went on a long walk instead of studying. By wild chance, I happened to notice a building that boasted a brass plaque with Mark Twain's name on it. He had actually stayed there. An inexplicable sense of homesickness swept over me. Twain was my favorite author—a fellow Missourian, river lover, and lover of words. I'd studied Huckleberry Finn in one of my English classes and became obsessed with Twain's masterful writing.

I stared at the plaque, running my fingers over the raised letters, overwhelmed that Mark Twain had actually been right where I stood. In my mind's eye I saw his Hannibal, Missouri home and marveled that from there, he rose to become one of America's best- loved authors and humorists. Funny how a simple plaque in New York City instantly ushered me back home. It also triggered a deep longing to see someone —anyone from Missouri. And since it couldn't be Mark Twain, Sam Gafner would do. Thus, heartache aside, I couldn't wait to see Sam.

That next Saturday around noon, I heard a knock at my door. I eagerly opened it to see Sam, predictably dashing and effortlessly cosmopolitan. Fourteen days later he was still working by day and touring the city with me every evening and on weekends.

On the last night of his visit, by wild chance, we got front row seats at Big River, on Broadway. This Mark Twain/Missouri thing was bizarre enough, but the coincidences persisted: at dinner we learned that our waiter had stayed a month at my neighbor's house—across the street from where I grew up. Then at the theater lobby, we noticed that the director's last name was Millen!

Inside, when the curtain opened, we were instantly swept back in time to a rough-shod Missouri, carried along on Jim and Huck's raft and strains of Roger Miller's aching melodies. New York had its irresistible charisma but Missouri held our hearts. We were spellbound and bound together by our mutual heritage.

All the coincidences and Big River made it hard to see Sam go. He'd become a comforting symbol of home and a constant companion. But Big River was over and Missouri Sam was gone and New York suddenly felt intimidating. I was doubly alone even though I knew Sam was returning in a week.

On the very day he reappeared, I happened to get a letter from Anne telling me that Sam kissed one of his former employees on an island in the Missouri River. *On an island, for crying out loud?* He was in the room when I read the devastating news, but I said nothing— unable to speak, what with the arrow thrust through my heart.

*Sam Gafner is a womanizer!* my heart wheezed painfully.

*But he spends so much time with me,* I countered.

*So what!* my angry heart yelled, yanking the arrow free. *The man never asks anything about you. All he does is tell you what he knows and what great things he's done.*

*He makes no effort to know you! You've never had even*

*one intimate conversation with the man!*

*Well you're the one who said Sam and I were in love!*

Remember?

*But that doesn't mean he's good for you,* my heart

countered, dabbing the wound with gauze.

*So WHY do I stay with him?* I pleaded.

*He's ridiculously handsome. He knows things you want*

*to know. He's curious and likes to explore the world like*

*you do. But the biggest reason you stay with this man who*

*keeps hurting you is that you've never learned how to*

*protect me.*

Hmmm. Good point. Now that I thought about it, I

realized I truly had no clue how to protect my heart.

So, I decided to take a stab at it. (Bad verb choice).

That night, after dinner in upper Manhattan, Sam and I ordered margaritas. I'd never had one and wanted to try it. Halfway through my drink, I announced proudly, "These don't affect me whatsoever!"

But by the time we were back in the dorm room things had changed. Sam instantly passed out on one of the two twin beds. I, however, still oblivious to my inebriation, wanted to talk. Really talk. About my hurt heart. I was set to plead it's cause—a good first step at protection, I thought.

"Sam," I whispered, sitting on the other bed. "I've noticed that we never talk. Except about geology, business, and physics. And you. You! You! You! Also, I'm sad you don't think I'm funny. I was born funny. How can you not laugh at my jokes? It's certain proof that you don't know me. You know nothing about my life and I'm tired of always being the one asking you questions about you. So, what do you think?"

Sam snorted and rolled on his side, sound asleep.

As it turns out, tequila makes me edgy. Mean, actually. And the next thing I knew I was throwing a paperback book—Einstein's Theory of Relativity to be exact—at Sam. As it flew through the relative space between us, I wondered where it would land given my terrible aim. I'd targeted his back. But the spine of the book crashed into his head. Sam rolled over, saw the book laying on the bed, picked it up, looked at the cover and calmly said, "I've been struck by the theory of relativity."

Then he rolled back over and began snoring.

Incensed, I stormed out of the room, slamming the door and went to the lobby to stand in line with the French foreign exchange students, all of us lonely and hoping to connect home. I tried to call Anne, but she didn't answer. Defeated, I staggered back to the room to watch Sam sleep. I had to fight off a strong urge to pummel him with my fists. This was a new battle for me—trying not to assault someone. I blamed it on the worm.

The next morning Sam was scheduled to fly back to Missouri. No time to talk about his trespass. So much for my first attempt to protect my heart.

The last weeks of the seminar flew by. We met with editors at *TIME Magazine*, toured the Condé Nast offices, and created a prototype publication. Then, suddenly, the dream was over. I had a job offer, but the meager salary wouldn't cover New York's high cost of living. Thus, I packed my typewriter and clothes and headed home. My first student loan payment was due, so I took a consulting job to coordinate public relations for the upcoming Governor's Conference. Ouch! State government again!

Sam graciously let me live with him above the flower shop. When he showed me the space he'd made for my clothes in his closet, I was grateful but devastated. I dropped my heavy backpack on the floor with a thud and my heart landed hard too—weighed down by being right back where I'd started.

Later that evening I walked to the river alone. I stood on the bank, throwing rocks in the rushing water, hoping to catch its momentum and a prospect of

something new.

Chapter 10


**It was challenging to live with Sam** above his ex-wife's flower shop, sleep in the same bed where he and Heather had slept and see my blood on the steps every day. The worst part though, was the employees' gossip—every morning, just to reach the front door, I plied through a thick residue of words spoken prior to my appearance.

Fortunately, however, when the Governor's Conference ended just before Christmas, I was offered a public relations position in St. Louis. The chances of getting the job were slim, but by some miracle, I managed to outdo the leading contender—the daughter of a famous Cardinal baseball announcer. I was stunned at getting the position, and so was Sam when he learned I'd be moving to St. Louis soon. Unfruitful discussions ensued. But I was unmoved about moving, desperate for a fresh start.

Logically, it was a perfect arrangement: The salary was more than I'd ever earned, the company would pay for a hotel room until I found an apartment, plus, I didn't start until mid-January. Emotionally, however, I was hurt that even at this juncture, Sam never talked about how he felt about me. But he did help me find an apartment with the intent to live there part-time until he could sell his flower shop, and I agreed to his plan.

Meanwhile, Sam and his friend, Eli, asked Harriet (autopsy decliner) and me to head to a beach after

Christmas—just one week away. On such short notice,

the only available hotel rooms were in Mazatlan,

Mexico. We would travel four days to be at a beach

for three. The travel agent advised against the plan,

but Sam, driven by goals, whether bad or good, was

doggedly determined to be ocean-side no matter what.

This required leaving on Christmas day. Harriet, ever a

sane woman, backed out at the last minute. But Eli and

I were swept into Sam's momentum—happy for an

adventure.

As it turned out, I helped Sam all Christmas Eve day

and night with a project for his client. It was freezing

cold in his office and consequently, both of us came

down with a ripping bronchial infection. Fevered and

exhausted, we rose at 4:00 a.m. on Christmas day,

picked up Eli, and raced to St. Louis to catch a plane to

Laredo, Texas. From there, after a three-hour layover,

we flew to Chihuahua, Mexico to spend the night at a

very questionable, low-budget hotel.

Completely exhausted, we all went to bed early,

hoping for some privacy and a good night's rest.

However, it quickly became clear this was not to be.

Through the tissue-paper walls, we could hear each

other's every movement, and as we laid our heads on

the pillows, Eli barely whispered, "Night Sammy. Night

Effie"—but it sounded like he was right there in bed

with us. Then a second later, as if planned, live mariachi

music blasted through our window from the courtyard

outside. There was instant yelling and wild singing—the

beginning of a wedding reception that lasted until 3:00

a.m. —right outside our window. Like it or not, we were all-night participants in a true Mexican tornaboda. Olé!

Fevered, exhausted, and near-deaf from mariachi, Sam and I boarded the rusted, dented bus at 6:00 a.m., with Eli behind us wrestling his submarine-sized duffle bag and camera gear. Travel is hard in a fevered deliri-um, but it's even harder with an anal-retentive lawyer— and Eli was one. He was exasperatingly thorough, hyper-punctual, brilliantly opinionated and packed like a pioneer going west. Even in my stupor, I perceived that unless you're the Trinity, it's not advisable to travel in threes. But it was much too late to turn back now.

We crowded together in the only seat left, amid peasant people with chickens in cages, one dog, and sparring children. Then, with a violent jerk, our road trip began. Four bumpy hours later, we were on a crowded train winding through the epic gorges and vast mountains of Copper Canyon. Sadly, I couldn't keep my head up or eyes open and fell into a deep coma-like sleep on Sam's shoulder. Once in a while, I'd rouse to see Eli stiffly wedged like a totem pole between two very obese Mexican women—one holding a screaming baby and the other breastfeeding her infant, both emitting profound body odor.

After seven hours, our last train stop was a tiny station in Bahuichivo—a speck in the vast Sierra Madre Occidental. From there, we took another battered bus to the tiny village of Cerocahui, where we spent two glorious days resting and one magical night watching

Halley's Comet cut a streak of light through the black, sequined night. There was no man-made anything in sight—just endless indigo mountains, the twinkling crush of countless stars, and the epic comet.

The next day, we were back on the train to Los Mochis, followed by three more bus trips to reach Matzalan. There, Eli drank the water, turned a horrible shade of grey and swelled to two times his original size. Sam and I parasailed, spent New Year's Eve in a loud Americanized bar and the next day began the grinding trek back home. Four days later I was living in a sterile hotel room in St. Louis, starting a new job.

Given all the commotion, it was no wonder I never even realized I was pregnant.

## Chapter 11

**When I showed Sam the pregnancy test results,** he sat down and buried his head in his hands, and from there, my life went grey. We exchanged words I can't remember which ended in the cold consensus that having a baby was impossible. I was the rope in a cosmic tug of war—pulled by Roe vs. Wade with its promise of freedom on one end, and my conscience on the other. But Roe vs. Wade won out because:

-Sam didn't offer to marry me or want to keep the baby

-I believed I couldn't work and raise a child by myself

-Five of my seven best friends had had abortions, and

-I was humiliated by being pregnant and unmarried.

So, there you have it. Appropriately, it was an exceedingly dark rainy night when I drove to Planned Parenthood alone. I'd told Sam he didn't need to come, hoping he would. But given an out, he opted to work late instead.

To this day, I'm stunned at how much I don't remember about the whole thing—where the clinic was or what procedure was used, the name of the doctor, or anyone's faces. But I do vividly recall how matter-of-fact everyone was, including me—reading a book about brain hemispheres during the procedure. And I vividly recall how time stood still when the doctor casually told me 'it' was a boy—as if commenting on the gender of a pet newt that died. I also remember sobbing uncontrollably once I got in the car. At home,

Sam said nothing, but took me to a Mozart concert.

The next day at work I had to leave a meeting and

race home. For two hours, I was doubled over in pain

and bleeding profusely. When I told Sam that evening,

he said he was so sorry. Then that was it. We never

mentioned one more word about the abortion. The

humiliating inconvenience was eliminated—tossed on a

pile of other such refuse—and we were greatly

relieved. We went on with our lives as if nothing had

happened: racing off to more client meetings, juggling

more project deadlines, squeezing in friends and family,

pushing to keep current. We barely noticed each

other, let alone the choices we made. Our blind

oblivion kept us from realizing we were completely out

of touch with each other and things that mattered most in life.

Within a year I was pregnant again (they were wrong—lightning does strike twice), but this time I refused to abort the baby. Five months into the pregnancy, I finally asked Sam why he never mentioned getting married (we'd been living together for nearly two years). He said he'd always wanted to marry me, but never found the right time to ask. Even after that conversation, however, he never asked. Finally, I mentioned it would be nice to have a ring and a wedding and Sam agreed. The ceremony was held in our three-room efficiency apartment, witnessed by a few friends, a few family members, and some resident cockroaches who decided to join the celebration.

The honeymoon was a six-hour drive to Swan lake to see the trumpeter swans and white-fronted geese congregate in masses. As it turned out, there was only one mallard duck. So we drove six hours back home and went to work the next day. Then, four months later, we had a beautiful, delightful baby girl—Jemma.

Within another year, we were pregnant again, and this time we had a strong, contagiously happy boy, Lucas. Life was a blur of incredible learning curves: making a home, raising two amazing children, building careers, maintaining property, and learning to be married. Much to my surprise, in motherhood and marriage I found untold joy and a sense of purpose beyond anything I'd known. Who knew?

The constant rush of activity was interrupted by my

father's battle with lung cancer and then brain cancer—

a horrifying assault that lasted three long years. Then,

one snowy night, right before Christmas, it was all over.

Just like that, he was gone even though I was still in

siege-mode:  The ghastly images and urges to be bed-

side persisted as my body failed to catch up with the

sudden shift-in-reality.  To cope, I crammed my days

with more busyness.

One day, however, almost two years after Dad's

death, I was strangely compelled to visit the

abandoned,1850's farmhouse where he'd spent his last

years writing.  Logic told me it was a futile thing—not

to mention eery.  Nevertheless, I found myself

cancelling meetings and driving for miles in the

country on the rutted, washed-out road leading to the neglected structure. Inside, yellowed papers lay strewn about the old pine floor. As I picked one up to read it, I was unnerved. In trying to clear his new ink cartridge, Dad had typed the same sentence over and over. And unbelievably, every page I picked up had the same message:

"When are you coming home?"

An eeriness I couldn't shake came over me. I knew that someone or something was speaking directly to me. An ominous sense of death filled the empty room and in fear I bolted out of the building and sped off in my car to escape it. But even though I'd left the premises, escape was not possible, because I was followed by a harbinger of death. Specifically, the death of self. Myself.

Feeling undone by all this, I began reading anything spiritual in nature—trying to find something to stop the sadness and unnerving morbidity. This ran the gamut of Christian Science, Unity, Hinduism, Islam, Buddhism, Mysticism, Judaism, Eckhart Tolle's Pain Body, New Age everything and even the Bible. I noticed, however, that there were great discrepancies among the beliefs and realized not all of them could be THE TRUTH. So, on my lunch hour one day, I dashed to the library to check out books on religions of the world. Silly me—I actually intended to do a comparative study and discover which one offered absolute truth. I stood in the Religion Section staring at the seemingly endless rows of books. I looked at my watch and realized I didn't have time during my lunch hour or my whole lifetime to read the vast array before me.

Taken back by the impossibility of my ridiculous idea, I asked this God I'd been chasing to show me his Truth. And to show me a penny—one single penny where that was being taught. I also specified no Jesus stuff — those people seemed stuffy and humorless. Plus, I hated gingham dresses with big pockets—what I believed the Christian women wore.

Thus began the search. I went to place after place (except Christian churches, of course) attending lectures and services, looking for a penny in every parking lot, lobby and auditorium, to no avail.

It so happened that Anne and her new husband were living in St. Louis, too. She knew all about my quest and repeatedly urged me to try a particular church she'd heard about. But I refused to of for three basic reasons: It was a Christian church, located near a huge shopping mall, and famous NFL football players went there. Despite those strong negatives, however, I felt a strange compulsion for the whole family to go there one Sunday morning.

It was a miracle we all agreed to go on such short notice and more incredible that we arrived early instead of late, which was our habit. No one was there yet, so I told Jemma to pick where to sit. In the dimly-lit auditorium, she instantly led us to four chairs in the ocean of empty seats. And there, balanced on the thin metal bar between two seats, was a penny! *The penny!* I

was completely stunned! *This nondescript, remodeled*

*warehouse was where God would reveal his Truth!?* Sam

looked as perplexed as I felt.

The speaker turned out to be a pastor. And all he

did was talk about Jesus, of all things! Yet, despite my

disappointment, we returned every Sunday for a whole

year—mainly because Sam and the kids really enjoyed

the music and the football stars. That was fine with me,

but I kept hoping the pastor would talk about

something else besides Jesus all the time. But no.

Every single Sunday it was Jesus, Jesus, and more Jesus.

Slow on the uptake, I finally began to realize The One

Truth I'd been seeking wasn't an idea, a doctrine, a

philosophy, or a human discipline. It wasn't something I

could learn about and then go on with life as usual.

The Truth was actually a person. God's Son. Who also

happened to be God. Who knew?

To my great surprise, I quickly developed a passion to

read the Bible, attend Bible studies, and listen to

sermons every day on Christian radio. I even

responded to an Altar call one Sunday and gave my life

to this Jesus Christ. It felt awkward, but at the same

time I knew without a doubt that I'd found The Truth.

And the next thing I knew, I quit work to be a full-time

mom. Then, a year later, Sam gave his life to Christ and

our marriage began to transform as we grew in our

faith!

All that was wild enough, but shockingly, I also

learned that when you give your life to Christ, God

immediately sends His Holy Spirit to live in you.

*Seriously?* I had just wanted TRUTH and assumed I'd read about it and move on. But here I was sharing my carcass with the God who said, "Let there be light." Wilder still, He was talking to me!

First, He had me start praying that Jemma and Lucas would be surrounded by believers in Christ. Not something I would have thought of, but I earnestly prayed it anyway, little knowing how God would answer—and obliterate our nicely planned lives.

*Per our plan*, we had just built our 'final' home— where we'd be for decades. It was strategically located just one block from the kids' new school. *Per our plan*, they left the public grade school and all their friends to make the change to a private school. *The plan* was for a one-time upheaval but then stability at a much better school. Jemma and Lucas had finally transitioned from missing their old friends and being the 'outcast' new kids. And now they had both made new friends. *The plan was in place. NO MORE MOVING!*

But one day, the Holy Spirit told me to cancel their contract for the next year as there was a slight change of plans—He wanted us to move to Boulder, Colorado! WHAT!?!? He might as well have told us to settle in Paraguay. This was in late July. School started mid-August. Understandably, Sam thought I was CRAZY. After all, *our plan was finally in place and working beautifully.* Why on earth would we uproot the kids again, leave our families, and move without any prospect of employment? Oh, and one more thing—

the Lord hadn't bothered to mention what school in Boulder.

Nonetheless, I was certain this was God. And I'd been reading in the Bible that faith pleased God—that He blessed those who just did what He asked. Sam was understandably displeased with this idea. Marital skirmishes ensued, but after much heated discussion, Sam finally agreed to meet with the headmistress of the kids' school and cancel their contracts. Then we had to tell the kids they'd be leaving their school—without knowing where they would be next (we didn't dare tell them about Boulder at this point). Unbelievably, they were much more accepting than we anticipated. Next, at Jemma's request, we sent her to a Christian camp for two weeks with her best friend. While she was gone, we took Lucas and his friend, Kyle, to Boulder. They had no idea we were on a scouting mission. They just thought we were taking a vacation.

Meanwhile, in the midst of all this, no matter what I read or heard, the subject of forgiveness was the constant theme—pelting rain that wouldn't relent. Finally, I'd had enough and thought to ask God what this forgiveness thing was about. I heard nothing but, somehow, I knew the Lord would answer me in Boulder.

Then, on the long drive there, I kept 'getting' a name. Over and over. It occurred to me it was the name of the school. I looked on the map of Boulder and was stunned to find a public junior high school by that name! Unbelievable! Sam and I were so excited and just knew the school would be amazing because God was obviously leading us there! The next day we took Lucas and Kyle on a drive around the city to see what it was like—which included nonchalantly driving by the school. Seeing it, however, our hearts instantly sank. The small building was run-down and in a very poor rural area. I fought to hold back a torrent of tears, asking God silently WHAT HE WAS DOING! We acted chipper though and took the boys to an amusement park. As they ran off to the rides, Sam turned to me with a look of endless perplexity and said, "WHAT on earth are we doing here Effie?!"

Tears streamed down my face. I felt responsible for this whole mess! I thought we were following the Lord but instead of glory, we were staring at dashed hopes:

a shack of a school, no job prospects, no connections—well, none except to God who was NO WHERE TO BE SEEN and NOT TALKING AT ALL..

After dinner that night, Sam stayed in our hotel room with Lucas and Kyle watching a movie and I went on a long walk to track God down. I walked and prayed and walked more and prayed more. My heart was aching and my head spinning with the obvious questions. This Boulder thing was so radical, yet I deeply wanted to do God's will. But mostly I needed some answers. Leaving our families, friends, Sam's work, our new home and life of suburban comfort wasn't so bad. But thinking of Jemma and Lucas in that tumble weed school—that broke my heart. I wrestled and grieved and finally told the Lord I'd trust Him even with our precious children.

Thankfully it was dark and the streets were empty, so I

was free to cry unnoticed as I roamed from street to

street seeking the Lord, determined to hear from Him.

Chapter 12


**At one point, I found myself standing at the bottom of a hill.** At the top was a large church. I was immediately drawn to it, like a moth to flame. The side of the building was enshrouded in shadows, but when I turned the corner, I saw the beautiful, softly-lit facade and a sign that read, "Sacred Heart of Jesus." In front of the sign was a stone marker, jutting through lush ground cover. Engraved on the flat surface was a drawing of two hands holding a fetus. A small inscription below read, 'In memory of those killed by abortion.' There was also a scripture from Jeremiah1:5, 'Before I formed you in the womb, I knew you.'

In a streak of searing revelation, I instantly knew that abortion was a sin against Almighty God. I was guilty of murder. Murder! That's what God called it. He had given me a son and I killed him. I sensed the inexorable, undeniable presence of God descend upon me. The weight of my 'choice' began crushing my soul in a death grip. Feeling I was about to vomit, I staggered across the street to a park. I grabbed a railing, managed to sit down on some concrete steps, and began weeping uncontrollably. Thank God I was completely alone. I felt thick black filth, wretched and impenetrable, in my chest. I wanted desperately to claw through my sternum and scrape it out.

Under God's holy, consuming gaze, all arguments, rationalizations, and cultural programing were completely obliterated. My sin was completely exposed. What I had previously considered to be a legalized necessity was now killing me. I felt I was suffocating. And somehow I experienced how my baby felt when extracted from my womb and murdered: Helpless. Desperate. And writhing in pain. I wept and shook uncontrollably, begging the Lord to forgive me, begging Him to deliver me. I knew instinctively something I'd never known until that instant: Jesus Christ was the only One who could save me, and I cried out to Him to please deliver me from this black torment.

Then, in a flash, the crushing stopped! I sensed a hand on my shoulder—the nail-scarred hand of the Savior, although I saw no one. Love I had never known flooded every microscopic part of my being. And I was

forgiven. Completely and forever forgiven.

"This is that 'forgiveness thing' you've been asking me

about." It was the Lord Himself talking to me, though

not audibly.

Completely undone, my heart cried out, *How can I be*

*forgiven for murder?!?!* I was compelled to pay some-

how—to make it right. His silent answer came instant-

ly, etching His Truth on my heart and altering my very

DNA: This is why I needed Jesus…to be set free from

sin.

For the first time I understood what Christ did on

that cross. It was no longer a cliché image, but a blazing

symbol of my freedom at His great cost. Stripped and

beaten, hanging there, Jesus took the punishment of my

sin upon Himself. He bore it so I would never have to. I couldn't articulate all this, but somehow I just knew it. And I would never be the same.

Suddenly, I remembered that ominous poem about the stone—that I wrote after kissing Sam the first time. Now, nearly 18 years later, I finally understood its meaning. It was God Himself trying to warn me. I clearly saw how a seemingly inconsequential thing—just one simple kiss—could lead to killing an innocent, voiceless life. My own son's life was "the mute attempt to stay afloat." The stone was my action: married yet kissing another man. No regard for leading a life that honored my Creator.

Then, in that split-second revelation, the park's sprinkler system triggered, spraying me with water. I leapt up and scampered down the stairs to a parking lot below. Clearly, the Lord was finished with the subject and shooing me on. I felt like a newborn colt on wobbly legs and leaned against a concrete wall to stabilize myself. Again, I heard His quiet, inaudible voice,

I gave you Jemma as a gift. And I gave you a second chance with Lucas to raise a son.

Who can imagine such relentless, undeserved kindness? Who can ever be the same when He floods you with mercy instead of punishment?

Basking in His love and seeing in His light, I suddenly realized the meaning of the Boulder move. *It was God's plan to remove the boulder of sin from me—not for us to move to Boulder.* I wondered why He couldn't have just told me that in St. Louis instead of taking us here to get the lesson. But He knows I'm a sucker for great stories and symbolism—plus we really needed a vacation.

So, this was my first walk of faith—following God even though *nothing* He was asking made sense. And oh, what a journey!

I was so excited about not moving to Boulder that I ran all the way back to the hotel. I couldn't wait to tell Sam. Filled with faith in such an amazing, faithful God, I asked Him to show me a clear sign ASAP so we'd know where He wanted Jemma and Lucas to go to school. And just in case the Infinite, Great I Am needed my infinitely finite input, I reminded Him that most schools were starting in a week.

That night I could hardly sleep. Unable to contain my excitement, I finally tapped Sam lightly.

"Sam. Are you awake?" I whispered.

"No. I'm sleeping, Effie." Sam mumbled groggily.

"Sam! I asked God to show us a sign—something we can't miss, a BIG sign—to show us which school He wants for the kids. I wonder how He'll let us know?"

"I hope it's not in Siberia. Work's hard to find there, I hear."

Chapter 13


**The next day, we left Boulder after a very late dinner.**
Our headlights traced the highway through the vast,
dark plains. We were all silent, but I was on 'red alert'
—expecting God's answer at any moment. So far,
everything I'd asked Him, He had answered in amazing
fashion! So, I trusted Him now more than ever.

As we were climbing a steep hill, we spotted a green
and white highway sign just ahead. I was strongly
compelled to see it and asked Sam to slow down. As
we drove closer, the headlights washed the reflective
white letters:

'W-E-S-T-M-I-N-S-T-E-R.'

When Sam drove past the sign I yelled, "Sam! Turn around! That's the school!"

"It's the city limits sign," Sam rebutted. "We're on the outskirts of Westminster, almost halfway to Denver."

"No. It's the school, Sam! Get it? It's THE SIGN from God—to show us where He wants the kids to be! You know, Westminster, that private Christian school? It's only about a mile from our house! I can't believe it!"

Lucas piped up from the back seat, "I can't go to a Christian school, Mom!"

"Dude! They'll make you a preacher," Kyle chimed in with deep concern in his voice.

Sam turned around and stopped. There we sat, the only people on the road, staring at this literal sign from God! A truly divine set-up that rendered me speechless. We would never have considered sending the kids to a Christian school. Yet now, because of all we'd just been through, we were 100-percent on board. Tricky God.

In amazement, I recalled the simple prayer the Lord had me pray just a few months ago—that Jemma and Lucas would be surrounded by Christians. In the process of answering, He'd completely uprooted our plans, removed my 'boulder' of sin, and reset the destiny of Jemma and Lucas. Westminster proved to be an incredible blessing for both kids, in ways we could never have imagined as we sat on the road that momentous night. And I was forever ruined to anything less than following this wild and glorious God.

## Chapter 14

**I have a stack of journals over a foot tall**, all filled with stories of how God himself has personally marked my days and completely transformed my life: every turn in the road,—challenging, but glorious, every walk of faith—arduous, yet vibrantly rewarding; every wrestling of self, the world, and the enemy—a victory in Christ. In every heartbreak, His comfort. In every lonely moment, His very presence. Through every dry apathy, His reviving streams of living waters. In every con-founding confusion, His beautiful, freeing clarity.

And here's where this story ends—which is also a beginning:

At one point, after walking intimately with the Lord for a decade, I sensed the Holy Spirit calling me to leave a marriage ministry where I'd worked for seven years. I was sad to go and perplexed at having nowhere else to serve. After months of waiting on the Lord, however, I was finally led to volunteer at a Christian pregnancy resource organization, of all places. NOT what I had in mind at all!

Uninterested in this drastic, unappealing change, I postponed contacting the organization for a year. Instead, I busied myself getting our house ready to sell. But one afternoon while I was hauling things to Goodwill, the Lord convicted me of my deliberate disobedience. So, I made the call, went to the interview, and started my first day of training.

The minute I stepped in the building, the presence of the Lord was so strong I could scarcely keep from crying tears of joy. I knew I was doing exactly what God intended. There was an instant connection with all the women there—as if we'd all known each other for a lifetime. And there was a pervasive, intense sense of being on task…a tiny outpost in the city for the Lord.

I would be a Client Advocate, meeting with the women who came for our services: free pregnancy tests, free ultrasounds, etc. The training lasted for three months and was intense. At one point, I was alone in a room watching instructional DVDs. One in particular was about abortion procedures, explained by a former abortionist.

Within minutes, I was weeping uncontrollably, stricken by relentless waves of grief. Unable to take anymore, I turned the DVD off and cried out silently to the Lord, asking Him why this was happening since He'd already forgiven me years ago for having an abortion.

He answered in His gentle, loving voice—the one I'd trusted countless times over these many years:

You're right Effie. I have forgiven you.

Then why am I weeping and grieving again like that night in Boulder? I asked.

His answer was an explosion of revelation to my darkened heart, "I forgave you. But you haven't forgiven yourself." His words exposed something that had been completely hidden to me.

"But how can I forgive myself for murdering my son?!?" I cried out silently.

"How did you get saved, Effie?" The Lord asked me firmly.

"By faith. I believed Jesus is who He said He is," I replied, wiping my nose.

"Do you believe Jesus forgave all your sins and took the punishment for them?"

"Yes."

"Then don't play God, Effie. Who are you NOT to forgive yourself, when I have?"

I was in utter shock! My tears stopped, my heart no longer ached, my thinking had completely shifted and 10 years of arrogant self-condemnation vanished. Once again, the Lord had set me free! This was the beginning of deliverance from the pride of self-sufficiency. And I more fully realized how completely and continually dependent I was on Christ's redemption.

Through the next six years, I met with countless young women. It was challenging work but also a great joy because the Lord had filled me with His deep love for each one. They so reminded me of myself before I knew Jesus Christ: looking for validation in demeaning ways, trapped in deceptive cycles of bad choices, completely blinded to destructive strongholds. Because I'd been in their shoes, I genuinely related to them in the deepest ways. And I ached for Jesus to reveal His love to them and set them free—like He did me.

Sadly, many of the women were determined on having an abortion. We were trained to never judge or persuade—only to offer information about the different procedures and corresponding risks, and present other options for consideration.

By God's design, I saw most of the abortion-minded clients, being the only one of my coworkers who'd had one. This was terribly humiliating, but simultaneously rewarding because sometimes, when the Lord would occasionally have me offer my story, I was privileged to actually see a woman's heart soften. Yet I never knew what decision was ultimately made because my role was simply client intake, not follow-up.

However, the Lord changed that, one remarkable day. I happened to be walking through an open common area and noticed another advocate saying

goodbye to her client. The young woman was holding

her little boy's hand. He looked about one year old.

When I spoke, he turned, pulled his hand free, and

instantly toddled over to me, reaching high to be picked

up. It was as if he thought I was someone he knew. I

laughed out loud at his unabashed gesture, sweeping

him up into my arms. Oddly, the very second I held

him, I became totally overwhelmed by a powerful

sense—as if he was my own child. Crazy! I dismissed it

as some vestige of my empty-nest syndrome or a

maverick post-menopausal upsurge.

Just then the mother, in mid-conversation, checked to

see where her son was. She saw us and exclaimed, "I

can't believe he's letting you hold him! He never goes to

anybody like that." Then she did a double-take and pointed hard at me and all but shouted,

"Well no wonder he likes you! You're the one who talked me out of aborting him!"

I was completely undone! Speechless! I looked at the beaming, happy little fellow in my arms and silently praised the Lord so loudly that I felt my heart would burst and everyone would hear it explode! In that God-appointed moment, I stood as witness to His unfathomable mercy: I had taken a life—yet was granted a part in saving one.

Luke's gospel tells of Jesus entering Jerusalem on a colt, knowing He would soon be crucified. As the crowds gathered, Jesus's disciples burst into loud, exuberant praise over all the mighty works He'd done.

However, some Pharisees, who were displeased with the commotion, demanded that Jesus control His unruly disciples. But Jesus answered them saying, "I tell you, if these become silent, the stones will cry out."

I am one of those 'stones.' A hardened heart changed by Christ's love, crying out despite all my wretchedness, in the glorious fullness of His unfathomable redemption,

"HALLELUJAH ANYWAY!"

## I Thirst

Fevered for Truth,
we search dry-streams
to dead-ends,
mistaking back and forth
with moving forward,
desperately searching
for even one drop
to stay the raging thirst
of body, mind, and soul.

On sun-scorched roads
mirages dance and glimmer
always just ahead;
brazen streaks of hope
that promise life,
yet vanish in the deadly heat
of self-pursuit.

Combustive sparks ignite
in lashing, searing flames
that rage and burn
to windblown ash
and scattered cries for help,
which no one hears.

But
the One who listens,
hears
and runs to bring
fresh living waters:
His sparkling,
dancing,
brand new
Life.

Made in the USA
Lexington, KY
29 December 2018